FINDING LOVE EVERYWHERE

ALSO BY ROBERT HOLDEN

Life Loves You (with Louise Hay)

Holy Shift!

Loveability

Shift Happens!

Authentic Success

Be Happy

Happiness NOW!

Available from Hay House

Please visit:

Hay House USA: www.hayhouse.com®
Hay House Australia: www.hayhouse.com.au
Hay House UK: www.hayhouse.co.uk
Hay House India: www.hayhouse.co.in

FINDING
LOVE
EVERYWHERE

66½ Wisdom Poems
& Meditations

ROBERT HOLDEN

HAY HOUSE, INC.
Carlsbad, California • New York City
London • Sydney • New Delhi

Published in the United States by: Hay House, Inc.: www.hayhouse.com®
Published in Australia by: Hay House Australia Pty. Ltd.: www.hayhouse.com.au
Published in the United Kingdom by: Hay House UK, Ltd.: www.hayhouse.co.uk
Published in India by: Hay House Publishers India: www.hayhouse.co.in

Cover design: Amy Grigoriou
Interior design: Bryn Starr Best

Scripture quotations are from the New Revised Standard Version (NRSV) of the Bible © 2009 by Zondervan.
Rumi and Hafiz quotes are used with permission by Daniel Ladinsky.
Quotes from *A Course in Miracles*, copyright ©1992, 1999, 2007 by the Foundation for Inner Peace, 448 Ignacio Blvd., #306, Novato, CA 94949, www.acim.org and info@acim.org, used with permission.
"God spoke today in flowers" is used with permission by Ingrid Goff-Maidoff.

Cataloging-in-Publication Data is on file at the Library of Congress

Hardcover ISBN: 978-1-4019-5880-0
Audiobook ISBN: 978-1-4019-5906-7
e-book ISBN: 978-1-4019-5881-7

10 9 8 7 6 5 4 3 2 1
1st edition, March 2020

Printed in the United States of America

SUSTAINABLE
FORESTRY
INITIATIVE
Certified Chain of Custody
Promoting Sustainable Forestry
www.sfiprogram.org
SFI-01268

SFI label applies to the text stock

To my parents,
Sally and Alex Holden

And to everyone
whose work is
loving the
world.

CONTENTS

PART III: LOVING WHEN IT'S DIFFICULT

PART IV: LETTING LIFE LOVE YOU

FOREWORD

Consciously Walking Buddha Tickles Feet

What brings your eyes to any image, to a page, and your ears to sounds? Or your hands to touch? It is really a beautiful wanting: the processing of life and hopes the best we can. In a way, all we do is try to mount a horse (a Pegasus) that will take us higher into the sky (or deeper within) where beauty is so apparent we can stop for a while and rest, and be renewed in awe and thanks.

I doubt very much one will ever come to find . . . love everywhere if they are in a rush. What one can see from a speeding car, especially if they are driving it, and what one can see walking are worlds apart. And a mad rush can surely occur, be going on, if one is just sitting; that is, the mind can be in a rabid state overwhelmed by misunderstood relationships, or fear. And our relationships can surely include places and things, past events and anxieties about the future.

Once someone asked me if I knew of a Rumi poem that was worthy of a New Year's contemplation and resolution. And I then recited them this one from my book *The Purity of Desire: 100 Poems of Rumi*. It goes:

> Being in a hurry throws the key on the ground to a door
> I want you to enter.
> If you read my words slowly and out loud, they will
> help to pick the lock.

Yes, we want to "pick the lock" on our vision and on our heart so that we see and feel, receive and give more. Our every cell craves freedom. And what do we want "to enter": marriages, friendships, and valued commitments more deeply; and to be able to immerse more in our work, our play, and our surroundings, and benefit from efforts. I put in some geraniums the other day, and every time I walk by them they kiss me. What a deal! Gardening, the real gardening, is refinement, cultivation, unearthing the Self, compassion, the joy—"the kingdom of heaven"—within.

All is part of a swaying, a movement, a dance within some inconceivable (to most) divine luminous current or breeze. Fine for the leaf floating in the middle of a rushing river, and now even going over a waterfall, to think: *I might travel upstream for a while where things seemed less intense, and my destiny not so precarious.* A sweet delusion would that then not be? There is really a physics, a metaphysics to everything. One can put in motion actions that beget—desired—reactions. You can set yourself up to where not only a whole blooming orchard is throwing you smooches, but all the mountains, the rivers and fields, the stars, and all in the whole universe. In other words: Finding Love Everywhere.

I have been working with The Dhammapada lately for a project, offering a modern-day version of it. Some scholars might say The Dhammapada is the essence of Buddhism in words; it is 423 short verses that date back to the 5th century B.C. And if I were to distill Buddhism, and most all esoteric paths, into just four words they would be:

Sit until you know.

It does seem fair to say that if Buddha was asked how he became enlightened, he could have said, "I sat until I Knew."

Sitting until you know. That is really the Herculean feat of all feats. And there is a marvelous—and vital—humbling in that process, and an exquisite control/balance gained, that then allows God to fit into your hand, or glance, and be imparted. Otherwise, one cannot truly bless and deeply change the life of others. Though of course one can still do some fantastic good.

To repeat a little differently, the above paragraph, that I feel is at the heart of all transformation: sitting, contemplation. I think it is a very, very rare one who finds any great truths about life (or their self) and can share that treasure with others unless they have let solitude remove some of the veils from their eyes, and have given extraordinary service to humanity—or to our wondrous Earth.

And in that sacred knowing, in those greater truths, what does one experience? I think, some great and profound, blessed-cherished independence! A magnificent, radiant sovereignty. An eternal coronation of the soul—of self—by Self.

The sun wants nothing more than to be what it already is and could be satisfied with that for eternity. And look how beautiful a moon can be to share in that. Like the wise student, around the true teacher.

There is a precious sphere ever rising on a pristine world within, and ever rising in all space, if we can really, really be present. If we can accept and find the grace to see. And as Hafiz says in one of my books:

> It rises,
> a glorious sun,
> if one can sit quiet long enough.
> Seeing it, one feels, I now have everything,
> everything I could
> ever want.

Yes, yes, and yes: God's Beauty is that great, that astounding: that seeing Him, She, It . . . can make you completely satisfied. Just the miraculousness—the pure magic of existence—as perhaps a true scientist might who is not even a so-called spiritual-oriented person. But really, all is the Holy Spirit . . . manifesting—though incognito to most.

And I think we need everything. To feel an overwhelming treasure in our heart or hand—and the ecstatic gratitude that comes with that, or . . . a divine peace. Oneness. Wholeness.

May Robert's wonderful life and work and heart keep helping others to know that inherent in life is Light, is Love, the Son, the Sun that is indeed ever rising—moreover, indeed always there.

I love the idea of Finding Love Everywhere. And I *love* the idea of this little haiku mutant becoming more and more true:

consciously walking
buddha tickles
feet

I guess Buddha and Robert are in cahoots. And doing things consciously, well, I think it so helps us find—and rub—the magic lamp.

— Daniel Ladinsky
international best-selling Penguin Random House author
Taos, New Mexico, USA
June 2019

P.S. I don't seem able to put down the mic yet. Woke up this morning thinking this needed a P.S. It is in honor of The Happiness Project, which Robert is renowned for. And if Hafiz ever spoke at one of Robert's seminars, he (Hafiz) might have closed his presentation with these lines from one of his poems, which my own teacher so sweetly wanted me—and the world—to remember:

Have fun, my dear; my dear, have fun,
In the Beloved's Divine
Game,
O, in the Beloved's
Wonderful
Game.

Yep, it can get wild and crazy on our planet. So take care of your precious heart, and your evolving, ripening golden wings!

INTRODUCTION

Make Yourself
Spontaneously Available

I'll never find love again, I told myself. I was the last one to find a girlfriend. She was my first and only girlfriend. Now she wasn't my girlfriend anymore. She told me about a guy who wore a brown leather jacket. His hair was blond and wavy. My hair was dark and straight.

"There's plenty more fish in the sea," said my friends. They were trying to cheer me up. I tried to explain to them that my girlfriend wasn't a mackerel or any other fish.

I was so distraught that, in my grief, I nearly bought a pair of chipmunks.

Here's what happened. It was a Saturday morning, and I was in my apartment by myself. I had to get out. I hated being alone, so I headed to the city center with lots of passers-by to keep me company. I saw a pet shop, which I hadn't noticed before. I wandered in and looked around. I saw two chipmunks scampering about in a small cage. They were "On Sale." Twenty percent off. I picked up the cage, like it was a shopping basket, and walked over to the checkout. I was about to hand over my credit card when I suddenly came to my senses. I made an excuse and left.

The way I saw it, I was the only person I knew who wouldn't ever find love. And I wasn't going to settle for anything less either. No fish in the sea. No chipmunks. No sex without love.

I didn't have anyone to talk to. That's not entirely true, but it was nearly true.

My mum was in the mental-health hospital again. Her psychiatrist had ordered another round of electric shock therapy for her depression. She couldn't remember my name on my last visit. She didn't know I was her son.

My dad was homeless again. He had left our family home when I was 15 years old. He moved about a lot. I didn't have a phone number for him. The last time he called I was out (shopping for chipmunks probably). He left a brief message, but no number.

My work wasn't anything yet. I was trying my hand at writing. Me and my black Imperial typewriter. I'd submitted a handful of articles and short stories to various publications. No luck so far. Just lots of polite rejection letters. I certainly didn't want a career. My dad had had one of those. I wanted to do something I loved. Something to pour my heart into. I guess I hadn't found my purpose yet. I wasn't on fire. I was studying, though.

I carried a copy of the Bhagavad Gita with me. It was small enough to fit inside my coat pocket. I'd read it while waiting for the bus. I'd take it with me to cafés. The Gita was my constant companion. My friend Avanti had given it to me. It was my first spiritual book. I ended up underlining almost every sentence in it with a red ink pen. It was a great comfort to me.

The Bhagavad Gita translated means "the Celestial Song." It's a 2,500-year-old spiritual poem full of melody, metaphor, and deeper meaning. The heart of it is a dialogue between the young prince Arjuna and his charioteer Krishna. Arjuna, who is full of doubt and melancholy, turns to Krishna for guidance.

Krishna introduces Arjuna to three great spiritual paths: *jnana*, the yoga (or, philosophy) of wisdom; *karma*, the yoga of action; and *bhakti*, the yoga of love. He tells Arjuna that bhakti is the greatest path because love is wise, and love-in-action is our soul's highest purpose.

The Gita was my spiritual compass at the time. It pointed me to essential reading like The Dhammapada, the Tao Te Ching, *The Imitation of Christ,* and later *A Course in Miracles*; as well as the poetry of the Vedas, the Bengali saint Rabindranath Tagore, the

Persian mystic poets Jālāl al-Dīn Muhammad Rūmī (commonly referred to as Rumi) and Hafiz, the Lebanese writer Khalil Gibran, the Romantic poets like Keats and Shelley, and to modern poets like Maya Angelou, David Whyte, and Mary Oliver.

Over time, my studies helped to expand my views. Love wasn't just about romance, girlfriends, and sex anymore. I realized that love is the whole point of everything. Love is the heart of physics, the chief science, the artist's muse, the only real religion, the one great medicine, and the holy purpose of everyone's life.

Instead of searching for love, I decided to become the most loving person I could be. That's how I eventually found love.

WHAT WE LOOK FOR FIRST

> Love is the first thing we look for.
> In our mother's eyes. In the smile of a
> stranger. In the shape of clouds.
> In a new landscape.

As a young boy, my mother and father's love was everything to me. When I felt their love, I blossomed. When I didn't, I wilted. Like a flower that turns to the sun for light, I looked to my mum and dad for love. Their love for me was the vital ingredient that helped me to grow. At first, I didn't know that love existed anywhere else except in their loving gaze. I certainly didn't know that love existed in me.

We see love first in our parents' eyes, so this must be where love lives, right? Here I am! Look at me! Can't you see? As young children, we live and breathe in the energy field of our parents' loving presence. Their loving attention is our playground. It is the garden in which we grow. So long as we can feel their love, we are okay. But what happens when we can't?

When we don't see love looking back at us, we experience aloneness for the first time. Now we are apart from love. Love has disappeared, and we are lost. Something is missing here. A shadow is cast in our mind. Inside the shadow lives a baby fear, which I named "the basic fear" in my book *Loveability*. The basic fear is "I am not loveable." It is the root fear of every fear you will encounter in your lifetime, including the fear of not finding love, of losing love, and that love doesn't exist.

Now I am a parent, and I see how my daughter, Bo, and son, Christopher, look to their mum and me for the love they need in order to grow. When they look in my eyes, I want them to see that they are loveable. Parenting is full of daily tasks, but the only task that matters really is that our children feel our loving presence. How hard can this be? Well, if you are a parent, you know how hard! That's why every child carries the basic fear "I am not loveable," and it's how the quest for true, lasting love begins.

How do we find love and not lose it? Here's the first clue. My daughter was born at 10:41 A.M. on a Sunday morning. "I've never seen such big blue eyes," said my wife, Hollie. As I held Bo, she looked deeply into my eyes. Bo's gaze was constant. I felt like she was looking around inside of me. I was taking Bo in at the same time. *I'd like this moment to last forever,* I thought. What were we seeing? I firmly believe that Bo saw love in my eyes, and, most significantly, I saw love in Bo's eyes. When Christopher was born, it was the same. We both saw love in each other.

The eyes are the mirrors of the soul, say the poets and mystics. Like a mirror, they reflect the person who is looking into them. Bo and Christopher saw love in me, not because I am the source of their love, but because I am the mirror of their love. And I saw love in both of them because they are my mirror too. If you are going to find love, you must first look in the mirror. Not with eyes of judgment and hate, but with eyes of love. Look at yourself through the eyes of love, and you will see your original face—the face of love.

When Hollie and I named our children, we gave them the same middle name: Love. With this small gesture, we have given them a reminder, which they will carry for their whole lives, that they are made of love. Naturally, we do everything we can to make sure Bo and Christopher feel our love, but, more importantly, our real task is to help them remember that they are the love they are looking for.

IN THE WRONG PLACES

Come closer, my beloved.
What you are looking for is not outside you.
Nor will you find it inside you.
What you are searching for is YOU.

One of my mum's most prized possessions was her Viking 5 Metal Detector. She loved a good treasure hunt, and she had a knack for finding treasure wherever she went. Mum would go digging for gold along public footpaths, riverbanks, and local woodlands. She always came back with an assortment of buried objects including Roman buttons, Coca-Cola bottle caps, lead musket balls, Victorian pennies, and occasionally a real gold sovereign.

Mum also loved to go fossil hunting in the farmers' fields nearby our little village. The best time to go was after plowing. Come rain or shine, Mum was out there. She always came back with something—mostly ammonite fossils that looked like coiled snail shells, sea urchin fossils, and meteorites the size of golf balls. One time, I went fossil hunting with Mum and we found a tortoise in a hedgerow. We took him home, notified the local vet, and posted "Lost Tortoise" notices everywhere. No one claimed him, so he ended up living with us. We called him Fossils.

Mum was always searching for something. She loved perusing antique shops. She had a great eye for a bargain. Each year, we gave her the latest edition of the *Lyle Official Antiques Review* for her birthday or at Christmas. For years, she excavated an old Victorian bottle dump in the woods next to the house she was born in. Our garage was full of vintage perfume bottles, rare medicine bottles, and Codd-neck soda bottles—the ones with a marble in the neck—all perfectly preserved and worth a few pennies.

We are all seekers, and our lives are full of searching. Everyone you know, including you, is on a quest. It might be pursuing happiness, searching for meaning, finding your purpose, or chasing after success. What are you looking for? A sign from God? A healing balm? Someone to love? The search for the Holy

Grail is your story, and everybody else's, here on Earth. Your life is defined largely by *what* you decide to search for and *how* you seek it.

The search is important. We open our eyes. We start to pay attention to our life. We ask questions. We look for answers. We live with intention. My inquiry into love led me to Avanti; to the Bhagavad Gita; to my mentor, Tom Carpenter; to *A Course in Miracles*; to my wife, Hollie; to our children; to my love of poetry; to the Enneagram; to Louise Hay; to Daniel Ladinsky; and to all my friends. Everyone I've met on my search has helped me, in some way, to see more clearly what I'm looking for and how to truly find it.

Searching is not the same as finding. It's important that you know this. At first glance searching might look like finding. The word *search* implies, sort of, that you will find something. Some people search for love in all the wrong places, however, and they never find what they're looking for. For others, searching can mean they overlook what is already there right in front of them. As Rumi observed,

> You wander from room to room
> Hunting for the diamond necklace
> That is already around your neck!

Searching can be a form of blindness. It filters our perception. We seek but do not find. When I first read the Bible, I noticed that all four canonical Gospels told stories of Jesus healing the blind. I remember asking my friend Rev. Peter Dewey if this blindness was physical or something worse. Peter smiled and said, "Jesus's mission was to cure us of our spiritual blindness—not seeing that we are made of God's love, that creation is an expression of God's love, and that God's love is everywhere we are."

Early on in the Gospel of Thomas, which is one of my favorite Gospels, Jesus tells his disciples, "If those who lead you say to you, 'See, the kingdom is in the sky,' then the birds of the sky will precede you. If they say to you, 'It is in the sea,' then the fish will precede you. Rather, the kingdom is inside of you, and it is outside of you." In other words, love is everywhere you are.

At the end of the Gospel of Thomas, Jesus is asked by his disciples, "When will the kingdom [of heaven] come?" Jesus replies, "It will not come by waiting for it. It will not be a matter of saying 'Here it is' or 'There it is.' Rather, the Kingdom of the Father is spread out upon the earth, and men do not see it."

Jesus taught us to stop looking in all the wrong places and start seeing what's right in front of us. Mystics, like St. Catherine of Siena, accepted this holy invitation, and in doing so recognized that "every step of the way to heaven is heaven."

ENDING THE SEARCH NOW

My Soul whispered to me,
"Sweetheart, call off the search,
otherwise you will not see
that what you are looking
for is Me."

I had grown tired of searching. It had been nine years since I had first read the Bhagavad Gita. Now, here I was in India on a pilgrimage. I was traveling with four close friends who were fellow seekers. The plan was simple enough: find a guru and get enlightened. We met plenty of gurus there. You can always find several of them loitering outside every temple. They're as common as rickshaw drivers. Wherever we went, the gurus saw us coming—the spiritual tourists in search of enlightenment.

We visited Bodh Gaya in Bihar, northeast India, toward the end of our pilgrimage. We traveled from Varanasi, the City of Light, on the River Ganges. It's also known as the City of Temples and the City of Death. Every year millions of people come to Varanasi to die. Their dying wish is to attain *moksha* in death. *Moksha* is a Hindu and Buddhist term. Simply put, it means "enlightenment and liberation." The corpse is cremated in full public view on the sacred river at sunset. The hope is that by dying here, in this holy place, one will be released from the wheel of rebirth and from the endless struggle of the spiritual path.

Although the distance from Varanasi to Bodh Gaya is only 155 miles, it took us two days to get there. The sun was burning hot. Our engine overheated three times, so we changed cars eventually. The roads were crowded. We had two flat tires. We encountered many obstacles along the way—especially cows, which are sacred in India. They stand in the middle of the road chewing on something. You can't force a cow off the road, as it's bad karma to do so. You have to wait until they decide to go. Cows in India are passive-aggressive. Like the gurus, they work the spiritual thing to their advantage. When you travel in India, you get there when you get there.

The morning after we finally arrived in Bodh Gaya, I went straight to the Mahabodhi Temple. I didn't go into the temple. I was looking for the Bodhi tree that stands outside. This tree is called the Sri Maha Bodhi. It is believed to have been propagated from the original Bodhi tree, the one that Siddhartha Gautama sat under 2,500 years ago. I wandered around the temple and found the tree. Hardly anyone was there—just a few monks wrapped in burgundy and saffron robes, sitting in morning meditation.

I laid out my prayer mat near the base of the Bodhi tree. I emptied my rucksack, rolled it up, and used it as a makeshift cushion. The ground was bare and hard. I sat in a full lotus posture, which, once you get the hang of it, is good for stability and comfort. I'd brought with me my journal, two pens, a copy of The Dhammapada, my water bottle, and several spirulina health bars. They tasted awful, but are meant to be good for you. I faced toward the sun. It was already hot. I was grateful for the shade of the Bodhi tree, as I planned on staying there for the rest of the day.

Later that morning, I was visited by a scrawny gray cat. He had the most beautiful topaz-blue eyes. He stood before me and stared up at me. "What do you want, cat?" I asked. He kept staring at me. I had nothing to give him. He didn't want my spirulina bars. Eventually, he curled up against my left leg. I was glad for the company. We meditated together. As I closed my eyes, the first thing I saw was his clear blue eyes looking at me.

"What's your name?" I asked the cat. He stayed with me for several hours. "I can't keep calling you 'cat,'" I said. So, I called him Siddhartha.

The story goes that Siddhartha Gautama arrived in Bodh Gaya after many years of seeking enlightenment. He had met many gurus and walked many paths. He mostly practiced asceticism, self-denial, and abstinence. Despite making great progress, Siddhartha felt a gap between where he was and where he wanted to be. At Bodh Gaya, he sat in meditation under a sacred fig tree for three days and three nights. This place became known as the Immoveable Spot. Here is where Siddhartha renounced the search for enlightenment. However, on the third day, Siddhartha experienced what he had been searching for. The fig tree was transformed into a Bodhi tree. Siddhartha was reborn as the Buddha, which means "the Awakened One."

As I sat beneath the Bodhi tree, I imagined myself ending the search just like Siddhartha had done. I was disillusioned with my own spiritual progress. I was grieving the death of my dad, whose alcoholism finally killed him. I felt utterly helpless about my mum and her recurring bouts of depression. I had a daily spiritual practice that I did without fail. I also had a library of spiritual books at home. I was a voracious reader who couldn't wait to get to the end of each book I read. Like Bono sings in the famous U2 song, I believed in the Kingdom Come, but despite my own best efforts, I still hadn't found what I was looking for.

That day beneath the Bodhi tree, with Siddhartha beside me, I prayed for a miracle. "Dear God, I need a miracle. I'm tired of trying this hard. There must be a better way." It felt good to say the prayer aloud. I packed up my rucksack, said farewell to Siddhartha, and made my way back to the hotel. On the way, I met a young boy selling Bodhi seed malas (prayer beads). He'd made them from seeds collected under the Sri Maha Bodhi tree. I bought ten malas from him, one for me, one each for my fellow travelers, one for my mum, and a few extra for friends back home. I still have my mala beads, 25 years later. They are my reminder of the moment I finally gave up the search.

Why wait for Heaven?
Those who seek the light are merely
covering their eyes.
The light is in them now.
Enlightenment is but a recognition,
not a change at all.

A COURSE IN MIRACLES (W-PI.188.1:1–4)

Finding *A Course in Miracles* was an answer to a prayer for me. One week after returning from my Indian pilgrimage, I went to a mind-body-spirit festival in London. As I wandered around the big hall, I came across an esoteric bookstall with an interesting collection of old, new, and rare books. The old man running the stall wore a crumpled tweed jacket and small round spectacles. His hair was white and wavy. He had piled books onto tables in no particular order. He was busy shuffling around, putting his books back in their place after they'd been thumbed.

As I searched through his books, I came across a large green paperback with gold lettering. It was the Penguin Arkana edition of *A Course in Miracles*.

"What's this book about?" I asked the old man.

"It's about love and fear," he replied.

"Oh, a bit like *War and Peace*."

The old man didn't reply.

"Have you read it?" I asked.

"Not all of it."

"Would you recommend it?"

"It says it's about 'a journey without a distance, to a goal that has not changed,'" he said, as he turned his back to me and wandered off to the other side of the stall.

I knew I was going to buy *A Course in Miracles* before I opened it. I guess I'm a sucker for a good title. I flicked open the book, and sure enough, I landed on the exact page in Chapter 8, Part VI: The Treasure of God, where it talked about "a journey without distance." On the back cover, it reads, "According to the *Course*, 'miracles occur naturally as expressions of love,' and all we have to do to experience miracles instead of problems in our own lives is to be aware of love's presence."

A Course in Miracles is a big book. It's more than 1,200 pages and 500,000 words long. Hence my *War and Peace* remark, which the old man didn't acknowledge. The *Course* is written in old-style Christian English and is full of iambic pentameter, which is the meter that William Shakespeare often used. It's a book of spiritual poetry presented in prose form. Many years later, I wrote a book called *Holy Shift!* in which I took 365 passages from the *Course* and presented each one as a poem. I didn't change the words or the grammar; I simply changed the layout. Paragraphs became poems, and *Holy Shift!* is now a favorite study companion for *Course* students worldwide.

The Introduction to the *Course* is only one page long. As I read it, I was struck by these two sentences: "The course does not aim at teaching the meaning of love, for that is beyond what can be taught. It does aim, however, at removing the blocks to the awareness of love's presence, which is your natural inheritance." Note it doesn't say "blocks to love's presence"; rather, it says "blocks to the awareness of love's presence." As I was to learn later on, the *Course* teaches that love has no opposite and therefore it cannot be blocked; only the awareness of it is. According to the *Course*, love is everywhere.

I bought the *Course* from the old man. When I got it home, I started to study it. Honestly, I found it hard going and couldn't get my head around it. So, initially I simply flicked it open and read passages at random. Here's one of the first passages I read, which I've arranged in poem form for you:

> Your task is not to seek for love, but merely
> to seek and find all of the barriers within
> yourself that you have built against it.
>
> It is not necessary to seek for what is true,
> but it *is* necessary to seek for what is false.
> Every illusion is one of fear, whatever form

it takes. And the attempt to escape from
one illusion into another must fail.

If you seek love outside yourself you can be
certain that you perceive hatred within,
and are afraid of it.

Yet peace will never come from the illusion
of love, but only from its reality.
(T-16.IV.6:1–6)

Here was my confirmation that now was the time to end the search. It was also an invitation for me to identify the barriers within that were blocking my awareness of love's presence. After some initial resistance, I got over myself, and I started to study the *Course* daily. It is, as the old man said, a book about love and fear. The *Course* teaches us not to search for love, but to identify with love. Our true nature (the Self that God made) is love. "You are the work of God, and His work is wholly lovable and wholly loving. This is how a man must think of himself in his heart, because this is what he is," says the *Course* (T-1.III.2:3–4).

What are the blocks to the awareness of love's presence? The first block is the *ego*, which is the idea that you are a separate "I" alone in the universe—separate from others, separate from God, and separate from love. This "optical delusion of separation," as Einstein called it, is what causes us to search outside of ourselves. And to repeat what the *Course* says, "If you seek love outside your-self you can be certain that you perceive hatred within, and are afraid of it" (T-16.IV.6:5). The words *hatred within* are a reference to the basic fear, which is "I am not loveable."

The *Course* teaches that the ego's basic doctrine is "Seek but do not find." The ego is afraid to find love for many reasons. This is true, isn't it? "I'm not afraid to find love," my friend once told me. She hadn't been in a romantic relationship for seven years. When she finally met the love of her life, everything was roses for about two weeks. Then, one by one, her fears emerged from the shadows of her mind—the fear of being unworthy, the fear of rejection, the fear of getting hurt, the fear of everything going wrong again! It's the same with God as it is with lovers. No one really wants to find God, not while we still carry within us the basic fear of not being loveable.

We look either through eyes of love or eyes of fear, teaches the *Course*. When you carry the basic fear "I am not loveable," you project this fear onto all your relationships, and that makes you even more afraid. Similarly, if you're holding on to wounds from the past, you will project this pain, doubt, and anger onto everyone who comes close to you now. You can't carry a grievance and let love in. You have to let the grievance go so as to make room for love. Until you forgive the past, you will be afraid to show up in the present. If you're not present, it's not possible to find love where you are.

Studying the *Course* has helped me to identify many blocks to the awareness of love's presence. I learned that if you want to find love, you have to give up your plan for finding love. Everyone has a plan for how love should show up in their life. I know I did. I wanted to get married and live happily ever after. That didn't happen in my first marriage. I wanted children before I was 30. That didn't happen either. I've made friends and lost friends. I wanted fame and fortune. I wanted to find God. None of it happened the way I thought it would, but it has happened in its own way. You have to give up your plan and let love lead the way.

I studied the daily lessons in *A Course in Miracles* for a year. When the year was over, I'd reached the end of another book. What now? I said a prayer asking for another miracle. Three days later, I received a package in the mail from my friend, the reverend and author, Diane Berke in New York. It was a recording of a talk by Tom Carpenter. Who was Tom Carpenter? I hadn't heard of him before. Later that morning, I sat down to listen to some of Tom's talk. I listened all the way through without stopping. What I heard changed my life forever.

IT'S EVERYWHERE YOU ARE

> "Love is everywhere," the Angel told me.
> "The real question is, Where are you?"

No one who searches for love can find love by themselves. We all need someone to help us open our eyes and teach us how to see. Who is that person for you? Who taught you how to find what you're searching for? Everyone needs a lover, an angel, or a mentor—traditionally called a *seer*. Rumi is the most prolific author of love on our planet, with his 3,500 odes; 2,000 rubaiyat, or quatrains; and the epic *Mathnawi*, which is made up of six books of poetry with 25,000 verses. Rumi's great outpouring came after he met Shams of Tabriz, his spiritual mentor. It was Shams who opened Rumi's eyes—after that, there was no end to his seeing.

Tom Carpenter has been my mentor for the last 25 years or so. By my calculation, we've spent at least 18 months as guests in each other's homes in Kauai, Seattle, Oxford, and London. When we're together, we begin each day in meditation and then we spend the rest of the day talking about the big stuff—happiness, forgiveness, Christ, the Kingdom of Heaven, God, and love. Over the years, we've presented several gatherings together. We've made a film called *A Dialogue on Forgiveness*. My book *Holy Shift!* is dedicated to Tom, and Tom's book *The Miracle of Real Forgiveness* is dedicated to me.

Tom is a not a front-page guru. He hasn't written a *New York Times* bestseller. He doesn't have a spiritual career. He teaches a weekly class at the local library, which focuses on the teachings of *A Course in Miracles*. Tom is an ordinary mystic. And although his life looks ordinary, the way he sees things is anything but. Over the years, I've watched in awe as Tom has helped people to open their eyes and find what they're looking for. Everyone who has met Tom will tell you about how he looks into your soul with his kind crystal-blue eyes. His loving presence is a sacred experience. Why is Tom my mentor? *Because when Tom speaks about love, it's as if love is speaking directly to you.*

One evening, Tom and I were taking a walk along Hanalei Bay on Kauai. We had come down to the bay after a daylong public gathering, hosted by Tom and his wife, Linda. Once again, I had witnessed a room full of people be transformed by Tom's loving awareness.

"How do you do it, Tom?" I asked.

"Do what?" he said, with a smile.

"How do you love people like that?"

"Like what?"

"So that they feel seen," I said.

"Umm," said Tom.

"So that they are transformed by love," I said.

"Umm," he said again.

Umm is one of his favorite words, if you can call it a word.

"You must know how you do it!" I said.

"I do one thing and one thing only," Tom replied.

"What's that?"

"I make myself spontaneously available to the love of God."

This phrase—*spontaneously available*—sounded lyrical and sweet to me. I had not heard it before, and I knew I would not forget it. I had been given an invaluable key. "What exactly do you mean, Tom?" I asked.

Tom told me that in order to love and be loved, you must be willing to ask love to show you how. "We try to love ourselves without love's help," he said. "We try to find love without love's help. We try to love one another without love's help. But, without love's help, we suffer."

Tom encouraged me to appoint Love as my spiritual teacher. I did this by making myself spontaneously available to the Love of God. Being spontaneously available has been my spiritual practice ever since. It's not a technique; it's an intention. In my daily journal, I write at the top of each page: "Love, what do you want me to know today?" I tune in to Love. I listen to Love's voice. I take notes. Similarly, each morning I pray, "Dear Love, show me how to love my daughter, Bo, today," and, "Dear Love, show me how to love my son, Christopher, today." Love is intelligent, and Love knows how to love.

Being spontaneously available begins with emptying out everything in your rucksack—in other words, emptying your mind of learned theories and theses about what love is. The mystics call this practice *kenosis*. The less noisy your mind is, the easier it is to hear the voice for Love. Through this practice of being spontaneously available to Love, I started to write poetry on a regular basis. I didn't mean to do it. It happened naturally. Many of the poems in this book appeared on pages in my daily journal while I was listening to the voice for Love.

"Who do you think the voice for Love belongs to?" Tom asked me.

"Umm," I said, borrowing his favorite word for a moment.

"The voice for Love is your original voice," he said.

"Umm."

"Love is your original mind."

"Umm."

"Love is what you are."

As I write this introduction to *Finding Love Everywhere,* Tom is putting the finishing touches to his new book *Let Love Find You.* We're looking forward to hosting a joint celebration for the launch of our books.

By being spontaneously available to love, you let love find you. You also become more open and receptive to finding love everywhere. It's inevitable that you will find love and love will find you because you are now coming out of hiding and you are now willing to accept, in all humility, that you are the love you have been looking for.

A NOTE ABOUT POETRY

I didn't have much time for poetry when I was young. Maybe I was in too much of a hurry. My mum used to tell me I was born with fast genes. I was full of muscle, headstrong, and driven by ambition back then. Fortunately for me, one poem after another found their way through my defenses and came to my rescue. Slowly, but surely, I began to see that inside each poem there was a gift waiting for me. A gift to help open up something inside of me—a new awareness, an epiphany, a cure for loneliness, renewed courage, and a call to action.

Many of my favorite poems begin and end on the same page. Some are just a few lines long. Poets aim to use an economy of words for maximum effect. That's why a great poem can wield as much influence and power as an epic novel or great theatre play. There are single lines of verse that have somehow made all the difference to me. For example, when I first encountered Walt Whitman's *Song of Myself*, I stumbled across this line: "I loaf and invite my soul." These six simple words somehow gave me permission to slow down and enjoy my life.

"The mission of poetry is to inspire," said Hazrat Inayat Kahn, the Sufi mystic. That's why we recite poetry at inaugurations, blessing ceremonies, and other important occasions. That's why some poems turn into prayers. Nelson Mandela discovered the poem "Invictus," by William Ernest Henley, while in prison. It's a short poem, just four stanzas long. He committed it to memory. It became his touchstone. He recited it daily so as to access the inspiration and resilience he needed for his leadership and the challenges of the day.

Poems can often work like angels. They find you when you most need them. They bring comfort. They offer supernatural aid. They often appear out of nowhere. After writing my book *Loveability*, I became very tired. I tried to press on, but I couldn't. My willpower was failing me. I grew more tired each day. What was wrong with me? I began to panic. Was I ill? One morning, I noticed a file on my computer desktop. It was entitled "A Blessing." I opened it and there was a poem called "A Blessing for One Who Is Exhausted" by John O'Donohue. This poem offered me precisely the wise counsel I most needed at the time. Where did it come from? Who sent it to me? I searched my mail Inbox folders "Junk," "Trash," "Archive." There was nothing there. It came from nowhere.

Some poems become lifelong friends. You turn to them when you need good company. They help you to pay attention to your life. They encourage you to stay faithful to yourself. There are several poems I wouldn't want to live without. Each time I read "What to Remember When Waking," by David Whyte, its rhythm and rhyme help me to re-center myself. My life is better for having met this poem. It knows me by heart. It helps me to remember and re-commit to what is sacred to me.

The very best poems inspire some sort of action. Mary Oliver's poem "The Summer Day" is a fine example. It's another poem that begins and ends on the same page. In it she paints a picture of a day when she lay down in a field and watched a grasshopper eat, wash and fly away. She loafed and invited her soul. She was idle and blessed. Doing nothing, she was fully alive. At the end of her poem she turns her gaze towards us and asks, "Tell me, what is it you plan to do with your one wild and precious life?" Best to stay away from dangerous poems like this one if you will not rise up and live.

The poems I have written for *Finding Love Everywhere* come in all shapes and sizes. Most of them begin and end on a single page. They are meditations with lyrics. They invite you to be wise, to choose love, and to live your most authentic life.

PART I

LOOKING FOR LOVE

Love is everywhere you are.
Turn yourself around before the angels,
as Mary did. Look again with the
eye of the heart and see what
love sees.

Most of the poems I wrote for this book were written in handmade journals from Assisi, Italy. I always buy a batch of journals each time I make a pilgrimage there to walk in the footsteps of St. Francis and St. Clare. I try to bring enough home to last me until my next pilgrimage. Sometimes I run out. Fortunately, I have friends who arrange for emergency supplies to be sent to London.

Assisi is full of poetry. I've spent hours writing poems in the church of San Damiano and in the forest behind the Hermitage of Carceri. At home in London, my Assisi journals help me stay close to the love that is everywhere.

St. Francis of Assisi took many pilgrimages in his lifetime. While St. Clare, who was one of the first followers of St. Francis, was happy to stay at home in her cloister at San Damiano, St. Francis was always on a journey to somewhere—Rome, Spain, Morocco, Egypt, and Jerusalem. As a young man, Francesco Bernardone was a pleasure seeker. He sought glory in war. With his conversion at San Damiano, however, Francesco ended his search. He no longer took pilgrimages in search of something. His purpose now was to spread the Gospel. He wasn't looking for love; he bought the love with him. St. Francis didn't take pilgrimages to find something. My poem "Bring Love" is the first poem in Part I. It was written in Assisi, and I think of St. Francis each time I read it.

The main aim of St. Francis's life was to experience Christ Consciousness. He wanted to be anointed by Divine Love. Jesus Christ was St. Francis's example and mentor. In the Gospel of John, Jesus proclaims, "God is Love." In the Farewell Discourses of the Gospel of John, when Jesus is preparing to leave, he tells his disciples: "Ye shall seek me, and as I said unto the Jews, 'Whither I go, ye cannot come,' so now I say to you. A new commandment I give unto you: that ye love one another, as I have loved you, that ye also love one another. By this shall all men know that ye are my disciples: if ye have love one for another."

St. Francis took the New Commandment to heart. He believed that if he could love everyone, he would find what he was looking for. Over time, St. Francis realized that love leaves no one out, not a single soul—not lepers, not animals, not stones, not anything. He was transformed by a cosmic, nondenominational love that he shared with Brother Sun and Sister Moon, as well as with Brother Wolf and Sister Death. His first language was love, which is how creation speaks to itself. It's how he was able to deliver his Sermon to the Birds. I explore the universal language of love in my poem "Common Love."

St. Francis is the man who found love everywhere. That's how I describe him to students who come with me on my pilgrimages to Assisi. His main practice was to empty himself of everything that is not love. Thus, he practiced kenosis like other Christian mystics, which St. Francis referred to as Lady Poverty. St. Francis understood that love is the treasure we are all looking for. Love—the real thing—is more valuable than money, status, power, silks, jewelry, and anything else you can trade with on Earth. Love can't be bought. That's how valuable it is. Put love first, by practicing the New Commandment, and you will discover treasure.

"What you are looking for is what is looking." This is one of St. Francis's central teachings. By keeping his focus on love, he experienced the Oneness of Creation. He no longer experienced himself as being separate from what he was looking for. In the beginning, when we look for love, we think we are looking for a "him" or a "her" to love us. In the end, we realize that what we were really looking for was an experience of our heart, our true nature. "For where your treasure is, there will be your heart also," says Jesus.

The famous Prayer of St. Francis reads like a poem and is often sung. Although it was not written by St. Francis, as is commonly thought, it does beautifully represent him and his work. It begins, "Lord make me an instrument of your peace / Where there is hatred let me sow love." St. Francis turned himself into an instrument of love. Another one of St. Francis's central teachings is *"We should seek not so much to pray but to become prayer."* In other words, don't try to find love, search for happiness, or acquire abundance; rather, see that these are qualities of your true nature. They manifest naturally when you put love first.

St. Francis wrote one of the great Italian poems called "The Canticle of the Creatures." He often made up songs spontaneously while walking barefoot. His prayers were also lyrical and unrehearsed. He didn't write down much. *The Little Flowers of Saint Francis* is a small book that chronicles some of his writings, including his Sermon to the Birds. To understand St. Francis better, you have to be willing to love and keep on loving until you can see that there is no end to all the love in the universe. The following words, attributed to St. Francis, sum it up well: *"Preach the Gospel at all times. When necessary use words."*

BRING LOVE

Good news!
I just got my invite, and I trust
you did too.
The world is throwing a party
again tonight.
Planets and stars will hang like
bunting from the ceiling.

Bees will bring honey.
Cows and goats will bring milk.
Flowers will bring perfume.
And each worm will bring a doily
made of silk.

Vegetables and minerals will sit
on every table.
Grapes will make wine.
Whales will recite sonnets from
the deep.
And dolphins will leap and play
and have a great time.

The wind and trees will make
music.
Birds, like the lark and the dove,
will sing.
All God's creatures will bring a
little something.
And humans will bring love.

THE I AM

Put a picture of Jesus
in your wallet, next
to your Amex card,
your dollar bills, and
everything else in
there.

Put a tattoo of the Buddha
on your body somewhere.
No one need ever know,
unless you want them
to.

Print the word *love*
on your T-shirt.
Hang a sacred heart on
the kitchen wall.
Wear holy beads like
jewelry.

Download the Rumi app
for poetry on the go.
Buy angels, buy crystals,
buy a rainbow, and a
Tibetan bowl. Get all the
spiritual stuff you
can.

Do what you must do
until you can trust that
you are the Christ, the
Buddha, the love, and
that you are the
I AM.

COMMON LOVE

Do cypress trees in Tuscany discuss things
together in Italian?

Do the great big black birds in Osaka sing
to each other in Japanese?

Do busy fish in the sea ever debate their
nationality?

And what about wild orchids in Ladakh?
Do they ever argue behind each other's backs?

Does an artichoke in Jerusalem prefer to be
eaten by a Jew or a Muslim?

Does a bumblebee in Spain share the same
philosophy as a bee in Gibraltar?

Does a coffee bean in Guatemala feel akin to
cousin beans in Argentina or Brazil?

And what about us, my friend?
Will we ever truly live together?

We humans, you and I, will we learn
to love before we die?

ACTING HOLY

Before, when I wanted to
talk with God,
I would cleanse myself,
light candles,
adopt a good posture,
meditate, pray,
offer some sacrifice,
get serious,
and try to
act holy.

Now, I just say,
"Hey, God, have you
got a moment?"

DIVINE WONDERING

Sometimes
I wonder,
did
God create love,
or did
love create God?

Either way,
I suspect the
answer is
Yes.

LONELY PLANET

Odd one out.
Nagging doubt.
Administrative error.
Cosmic mistake.

A lonely planet.
On my own.
No direction home.
Where am I?
Meant to be.

Just a visitor.
Temporary visa.
Estranged.
In a strange
Land.

Only loneliness
For company.
Plenty feeling it.
Not just me.

An optical delusion.
Alone together.
Finding our way.
Back home to
the One.

RECOGNITION OF THE ONE

Love is the recognition
of the One that is dressed up
as your beloved,
as a stranger,
as your enemy,
and as you.

DIVINE GELATO

There's a rainbow over the duomo
in Milano tonight.
And I don't know what to do
about it.

My heart feels too big for my body
right now.
I could sing an opera, I suppose.
If I could remember how the tune
goes.

The La Scala orchestra is playing
a concert in the square tonight.

Love is in the air.

And all the men and women look
beautiful and Italian and cool.

I will eat gelato. That's what I
must do.

Gelato is the only way to eat up
all this love.

MEDITATE ON LOVE

Love, and let
Love be your
God.

Pray to Love.
Worship Love.
Sing to Love.
Meditate on Love.

Walk with Love.
Talk with Love.
Look with Love.
Listen with Love.

Dedicate your
life to Love.
Dedicate your
relationships to Love.
Dedicate your
work to Love.

Love, and let
Love be your
God.

ENLIGHTENMENT (A MEDITATION)

The Buddha was sitting by a campfire beneath a canvas full of stars one night. Some friends joined him. They began to ask the Buddha questions like, "What is life for?" and "What is the Self made of?" and "Is there a God?" and "How do we get to heaven?" The Buddha waited until every question was spoken.

Then he answered, "If you practice loving-kindness, you will know the answer to every question there is. Enlightenment does not bring love; love is what brings enlightenment."

YOU ARE THE LOVE

You are the love
you cannot
find.

You are the love
you most wish
to kiss.

You are the love
that will sweep
you off your
feet.

You are the love
you are most
afraid of.

You are the love
you are hiding
from.

You are the love
that will save
you.

You are the love
that is looking
for you.

HOW LONG?

So,
you've been
looking
for
love
for quite a while
now.

Tell
me this, my
beloved.

How
much longer do
you plan
on
looking
for
something you
can
find
everywhere?

IT'S ALL HERE

Love is here.
   Help is here.
Inspiration is here.
   Grace is here.

The journey is here.
   The gate is here.
The destination is here.
   Joy is here.

Heaven is here.
   God is here.
Peace is here.
Because you are
      here.

WHERE LOVE IS

Where there is love,
pain breathes,
tears smile,
hurt softens,
guilt loses its edge,
judgment forgets to judge,
fear is no longer afraid,
separation is over.

Where there is love,
You are there.

PART II

LOVING OTHERS
AS YOURSELF

Dear One, please stop judging yourself.
You are not on trial. There is nothing to fear.
This world is not a courtroom.
It is a garden.

I was traveling home to Oxford, having spent the month of August on Kauai with Tom Carpenter and his wife, Linda. I had arranged a two-day stopover in L.A. to visit my dear friend, the late Susan Jeffers, who was a psychologist and best-selling author.

"Let's do a book tour!" said Susan.

"Okay," I said. Susan got her car keys and off we went first to the Malibu Shaman bookstore and then on to the Bodhi Tree bookstore in West Hollywood. In both stores, there was a prominent display of poetry books by the front entrance. Each display had the same two books by the Persian lyric poet Hafiz. Neither Susan nor I had read any Hafiz poetry before. And now here he was in both places.

Susan picked up a copy of *I Heard God Laughing*, and I went for *The Subject Tonight Is Love*. Both books are renderings of Hafiz's poems by Daniel Ladinsky, an American poet and renowned translator (and the gracious author of the Foreword for this book).

We stood in the Bodhi Tree for over an hour taking turns to recite Hafiz's wild and sweet love poems to each other.

"Listen to this one!" Susan gasped.

"Okay, now listen to this one!" I countered.

We must have read 20 or 30 Hafiz poems out loud. We drew a small crowd. Several people recognized Susan. We really were doing a book tour! We were selling Hafiz's poetry. By the time we left the Bodhi Tree, the Hafiz books had sold out.

Who is Hafiz? He is the most beloved poet of Iran. He was born in the town of Shiraz in the early 14th century. His full name is Shams-ud-din Muhammad. As a poet, he took the pen name Hafiz, a term designated to one who has learned the Koran by heart, which he did as a young boy. Like Rumi, Hafiz had a spiritual mentor, Muhammad Attar, a Sufi mystic. In his lifetime, Hafiz wrote nearly 1,000 poems exploring every nuance of love. Sometimes he wrote as a seeker who was courting love; and at other times he was the voice for Love itself. Eventually, every trace of separateness was dissolved in love. "All I know is Love, / And I find my heart Infinite / And Everywhere!" he wrote.

Back home in England, I recited Hafiz to anyone who'd listen. I recommended *The Subject Tonight Is Love* and *I Heard God Laughing* to everyone who attended my talks and workshops. Hafiz covers all the bases. His poems address the shadow and the light. He is The Friend who shows us how to meet the whole human story—sun and moon, birth and death, suffering and joy, aloneness and oneness—with revelry, compassion, and love. I handed out Hafiz books to everyone on The Happiness Project and at Success Intelligence (my two projects), to the chiefs of IBM and Unilever, to fellow authors, and to those whom I suspected might make room for a poem in their busy life.

I first reached out to Daniel Ladinsky to ask for permission to include an excerpt from a Hafiz poem he had translated for my book *Be Happy*. I ended up asking for permissions on so many occasions that Daniel wrote back one time (I still have the e-mail) saying, "You are very welcome to a lifetime of free nonexclusive use of my Hafiz renderings!" Over the years, I have enjoyed a delightful correspondence with Daniel. His e-mails read like poetry—they are lyrical and full of light. He often drops in a spontaneous haiku. Daniel is always writing poetry. Not just renderings of Hafiz. His book *Love Poems from God* features renderings from 12 saints and mystics, including St. Francis of Assisi.

When Daniel is working on his Hafiz poems—he's published over 700 poems now—he keeps two stories of Hafiz very close to heart. In one story, Hafiz is asked by a translator what the most important quality is of his poetry that must be allowed to shine. Hafiz responded, "My poems lift the corners of the mouth, the soul's mouth, the heart's mouth, and affect any opening that can make love." The other story is about a conversation between a young woman and Hafiz. Here it is, in the form of a poem:

> Once a young woman came to Hafiz and said,
> "What is the sign of someone knowing God?"
>
> And Hafiz became very quiet, and stood in silence
> for nearly a minute . . . lovingly looking deep into the
> young woman's eye, then softly spoke,
>
> "My dear, they have dropped the knife. The person
> who knows God has dropped the cruel knife most
> so often use upon their tender self—and others."

Here in Part II, I start with a poem called "Love's Prayer." This poem was first published in *Life Loves You*, a book I co-wrote with Louise Hay, and it appears on the final page of the first chapter entitled "Looking in the Mirror." "Love's Prayer" is an invitation to drop the knife.

Tom, my mentor, opened my eyes. He showed me that every one of us is only ever doing one of two things in any given moment of our lives. Either we are *judging* or we are *loving*. Check it out. See for yourself if this is true. In *A Course in Miracles*, it is written that:

> Judgment and love are opposites. From one
> Come all the sorrows of the world. But from
> The other comes the peace of God Himself.
> (W-pII.352)

It's important to understand that *judging is not seeing*. When you judge yourself, you see only your judgments staring back at you. Your judgments are a *deforming mirror*, a term used by the novelist Anaïs Nin. She wrote in her journals that "every one of us carries a deforming mirror where he sees himself too small or too large, too fat or too thin. . . . One discovers that destiny can be directed, that one does not need to remain in bondage to that first wax imprint made on childhood sensibilities. One need not be branded by the first pattern. Once the deforming mirror is smashed, there is the possibility of wholeness; there is the possibility of joy."

The self you judge is not the real self; the self you love is the real you. What you judge is just an image. What you love reveals its true substance to you. Your true self is the self you see with the eye of your heart. It is only when you stop judging yourself that you can see who you really are. Hafiz has something to say about this. He says,

> But remember,
> For just one minute out of the day.

> With all the rest of your time,
> It would be best
> To try

> Looking upon your self more as God does.
> For She knows
> Your true royal nature.

The New Commandment that Jesus Christ offers in the Gospel of John beckons us to love everyone equally, without prejudice. Jesus Christ said he did not come to judge the world, but to love the world. In the three synoptic Gospels of Matthew, Mark, and Luke, Jesus Christ offers what is referred to as The Great Commandment. When a Pharisee tests him with this question, "Teacher, which is the great commandment in the Law?" Jesus Christ replies, "You shall love the Lord your God with all your heart and with all your soul and with all your mind. This is the great and first commandment. And a second is like it: You shall love your neighbor as yourself."

Here's the thing: we can't love our neighbors unless we love ourselves; we can't love ourselves unless we love our neighbors. Why is that? What you do unto yourself, you do unto others. When you judge yourself, you project your judgments onto others. For example, when you set yourself impossible standards as a parent, your children fail to live up to the standards you automatically set for them too. However, when you love yourself, your love flows automatically to others. Why is that? It's because it's all the same love.

In my poem "Falling in Love," I explore how love has no idea about pronouns. In love, the "he" and "she" melt into one. In love, the "them" and "us" become a "we." In love, the "other" and "I" are absolved. In love, we appear as we really are. The self-image we once saw in the deforming mirror is no longer there. It was only an image, not substance. In love, your true nature is revealed. As you love yourself, you want to love others more. As you love yourself, you make it easier for others to love you too. This is so because it's all the same love.

LOVE'S PRAYER

Beloved One,
You cannot judge yourself and know who you are.
The truth about you cannot be judged.
Put aside your judgments then,
for one sweet holy moment,
and let me show you
something wonderful.

See what it's like to be you
when you stop judging yourself.
What you judge is just an image.
After the last judgment,
you will know yourself again.

Love will appear in your own mirror.
To greet you as your friend.
For you are loveable.
And you are made
of love.

MEET YOURSELF

When you meet yourself truly
—in the absence of the unholy trinity of
shame, judgment, and fear—
you will find yourself to be
in the presence
of an angel.

BASIC FEAR

Love the fear
that hides behind
every other fear.

The basic fear that
tells you

"I am not loveable."

Love it with all the
LOVE in the Universe.

And watch it
disappear.

FROM THE START

I have been with you
from the start.
Not for a single moment
have we been
apart.

I am the Garden that you
never left.
I am your favorite
climbing tree.

I am the mind you once
trusted in.
You used to believe in me,
before you invented
karma and sin.

I am your mirror.
I have never judged you.
I am a holy affirmation.
I love you.

I am your singing bowl.
Your forgotten song.
Your divine mantra.
Your daily Om.

I am your meditation seat.
An experience of grace.
I am the meeting place.
Where angels meet.

I am a healing well.
I am your medicine chest.
I am a bed on which to lay
your weary head to
rest.

I am your pilgrimage.
I am sacred ground.
I am your church.
I am your treasure.

I am the holy site that
waits for you at the
end of your
search.

I've been with you
from the start.
Wherever you go, here
I am.

I am your friend.
I am your heart.

REUNION

I've been living in the right
half of my body,
using only my right hand
and my logic brain.
Being half a person isn't
doable in the long run.
At best, you have just
50 percent of
the fun.

I'm learning to live in the left-
hand side of my body now.
Bringing my whole self
together somehow.
Marrying the masculine with
the feminine.
So that giving and receiving
become One.

My intellect has befriended
my imagination.
My body and soul enjoy a
faithful correspondence.
To be fully human is divine.
It feels so good to reunite
Jesus and Mary
again.

THREE FRIENDS

The body,
the heart, and the head
are really three
inseparable
friends.

When two
or more of them gather,
it is impossible not
to experience
love.

FALLING IN LOVE

You can fall in love with the same person
for the first time at least ten thousand
times, if you play it right.
And that's just in the
beginning.

After that, you can fall in love with each
other more times than you can count.
And each time it will feel more like
love than before.

Eventually, you will fall in love together
as often as you want.
And even more than that, because
you won't have a choice
about it.

The last time you fall in love will
be when you finally let love do
away with *you* and *me* and *him*
and *her* and all of *us*.

In the end, only love remains.

Ha! It was love falling in love
with love all along.

LOVE IS A THIEF

So you say that you want to find love.
It's okay. It's what everyone believes.
But I see that you hide from love also.
Maybe you know that love is a thief.

When love knocks at your door, what
will you do with your locks and bolts?
If you let her in, she will cause havoc.
Be in no doubt, she will clear you out.

Love will give you everything you want
in exchange for every thing you have.
She will take from you what you hold
most dear. She wants your story, your
suffering, and all your fears.

Love's crime is cunning and wanton.
Love deals in identity theft.
By the time her work is done,
you'll have signed on the dotted line.
And there'll be nothing of you left.

ONE LOVE

I said, "Hey, God, let's talk about love."
God said, "I'd love a peanut butter smoothie."
I said, "Love is the greatest thing."
"The only thing," said God.
"I need to remember that more."
"I can help you with that," said God.
"Thank you."
"I like my peanut butter smoothie made with
almond milk," said God.
"I love that I can talk to you about everything,
God."
"You're always talking to me, even when you're
talking only to yourself."
"Wow, that's profound!"
"And when I'm talking to you, it's really you
who's doing the talking."
"That must be why we both like peanut butter
smoothies."
"Made with almond milk," God added.
"We're really just the same thing," I said.
"The only thing," said God.
"One love," I said.
"One love," said God.

HYPOTHETICALLY SPEAKING

Hypothetically speaking,
If your ego and LOVE went to bed,
got naked, and made passionate
love to each other,
only one would survive,
could come out alive,
to be able to tell
the tale.

THE ONE AND THE MANY

It is only through the
feeling of loving
and being
loved
that you will come
to see
the
One and the Many
faces of
God.

WITHOUT YOU

If
there was
no
sun,
things would be
very dull.

And if
there was
no
you,
there would be
no light.

PART III

LOVING WHEN IT'S DIFFICULT

Forgiveness is an angel you pray to
when you need a miracle to
save you.

Here in Part III, you will find a poem called "Into the Innocent Again." I wrote this poem in Findhorn, Scotland. It was a
Sunday morning at about 10:30 A.M. I was sitting outside the Blue
Angel Café, drinking a cup of coffee. The September sun was low
in the sky. There was a light breeze. It was warmish, but not cold.
I had been mic'd up already for my talk, and in about 30 minutes'
time, I was giving the opening keynote for a seven-day conference
called "Forgiveness: The Great Undoing." As I drank my coffee, I
asked God for some inspiration for my talk entitled "Forgiveness
as a Spiritual Path." I took out my notebook and wrote down
"Into the Innocent Again." It happened spontaneously. I opened
the conference with it.

In my poem, I draw a metaphor in which I liken the experience of forgiveness with a visit from an angel. It begins, "There
is an angel. / An angel who travels with you. / An angel called
/ Forgiveness." As with love, forgiveness is impossible to define.
There isn't a hard-and-fast science to it. You can't reduce it to a
formula. It requires willingness, for sure. But it is not just an act
of will. I've tried hard to forgive many times, but without success.

Like with love, forgiveness is not just a verb. You can't make it happen. You can't do it alone. The only way it works, it seems, is when you allow forgiveness to do the forgiving. That's why forgiveness feels like an act of grace, and like a visit from an angel.

During my keynote address, I presented teachings from *A Course in Miracles* on forgiveness. The *Course* teaches that forgiveness is unknown in heaven. Why? Because heaven is not a physical place; it is a state of perfect Oneness. There is no separation, no fear, and no conflict in Oneness. Hence, forgiveness is not necessary. Here on Earth, however—which is also not a physical place, but a state of mind—forgiveness is deemed essential if we are to keep on loving and being loved. We forgive to remove the blocks to the awareness of love. Through forgiveness, we find our innocence again. As the *Course* states,

> When I have forgiven myself and
> remembered Who I am, I will
>
> bless everyone and
> everything I see.
>
> There will be no past,
> and therefore no enemies.
>
> And I will look with love on all
> that I failed to see
> before.
> (W-pI.52.2:5–7)

Why is love so difficult? It's a question I often get at my talks and workshops. Indeed, that same morning in Findhorn, a priest stood up in the middle of my keynote, and with fists raised to heaven, he demanded to know why we suffer so. He let out a primal scream of resentment. He was angry at me, at God, and at some other people too. "I refuse to apologize for my behavior," he said, although no one had asked him to.

Again we ask why love is so difficult. The short answer is, it isn't. The longer answer is, we make love difficult. How so? We carry in our nervous system the basic fear "I am not loveable." This fear is what causes us both to look for love and hide from it.

The first step on the spiritual path of forgiveness is to forgive ourselves for being afraid that we are unloveable. The basic fear "I am not loveable" spawns every other fear, like not being worthy, not feeling beautiful, and being rejected by others. The basic fear causes us to be afraid of getting hurt in love. It's also why we make it so difficult for others to love us. When love knocks at our door, we peer through the keyhole, not sure whether to unlock the bolts or not. Standing there, we question love, test love, resist love, and oppose love. We want love to knock at our door, but for as long as we hold on to our basic fear, we have no intention of letting love in.

Sin is the word that, when uttered, sends a shiver through just about everyone's nervous system. It's the guiltiest word in the English language. The doctrine of original sin states that there is something fundamentally wrong with you. It goes hand in hand with the basic fear "I am not loveable." Forgiveness as a spiritual path aims to undo both the basic fear and the belief in original sin. How so? Forgiveness sees through fear and sin. It sees that just as original sin does not appear in the Bible (it was championed by Augustine of Hippo from the late 4th century), it was never real to begin with.

Tom Carpenter and I have made many conversations about forgiveness over the years. As I mentioned earlier, we made a film together on forgiveness, and our conversation continues to evolve. Just recently, Tom impressed upon me again how sin is learned, not real. "We are innocent until we are told we aren't. Afterward, we are still innocent, but we may have trouble believing it," he told me. Innocence is our original energy. It exists forever. Innocence is always innocent. Only our perception of it is scratched and obscured. With new eyes, however, we can experience our innocence again. Tom also said to me,

> Just beyond your belief in sin,
> is the awareness that there is no one in
> creation who does not love you,
> and whom you do not love too.

My poem "Surrender to Love" begins, "Admit defeat! / You've tried your best / To love and be loved / But without success." Love is not just willpower. Haven't you noticed that the relationships you try the hardest at are often the most difficult? It takes a higher power, which is Love Itself, to help us love and be loved. In my book *Loveability*, I share the joyful discovery I made that *love is intelligent*. Love knows how to love. Therefore, we can meditate on love. We can pray to love. We can ask love to help us. "God is love," teaches Jesus Christ in the Gospel of John. Let us pray to love then, in the same way we pray to God.

> Back to the School of Love I went.
> For too long I've played truant.
> "I resign as my own teacher," I said.
> "Then empty your head," said Love.
> "And let me show you what I know."

When love is difficult, it is tempting to give up on love. Of course, this is when we need Love's help the most. Every argument ends in love *eventually*. Love always wins in the end. Why? Because fear is temporal, and love is eternal. In my poem called "Love's Victory," I address my relationship with my dad. I was only 15 years old when he left home. My dad was my hero. Mum was not well, but Dad was our rock. Why was he drinking? I didn't know. His descent was gradual and then sudden. I never saw his war medals. I learned later that two ships he served on in World War II sank at sea. Like those ill-fated vessels, my dad went down with his own demons. He's been dead nearly 30 years now, and yet, his love lives on in me. *This* is love's victory.

"Black Madonna" is the final poem in Part III. It is a recent poem. I had just returned from a visit to the Montserrat Monastery, near Barcelona, Spain. I was there to teach a four-day retreat called Spiritual Growth & the Enneagram. Hollie made the trip with me, and each morning we paid a visit to the Black Madonna that is housed in the basilica at Montserrat. We would go early, at 7 A.M., before the crowds arrived. This was my first encounter with the Black Madonna, although I'd heard of Her in my early 20s. I knew, back then, I would meet Her one day . . . when I was ready to.

There are many Black Madonnas all over the world—over 200 in Europe alone. New discoveries of ancient Black Madonnas are still happening today. She is an archetype for our time. This one, in Montserrat, is a wooden sculpture that is believed to have been carved in Jerusalem 2,000 years ago. She sits inside a cylinder of glass, and Her right hand reaches through a hole in the glass. In Her palm, She holds a globe that symbolizes Creation. On Her lap sits the infant Jesus. Each time I stood before Our Lady, I became aware of a loving presence that was everywhere about me and in me. As I looked into Her deep, dark, fathomless eyes, I was innocent again. She showed me, with her boundless equanimity, that there is nothing love cannot handle. Love is not afraid of the world.

MY LINES

I
am an
actor.

I
am dying
on
stage.

I
don't know
my
lines.

I've
lost the
plot.

Only
love can
save
me
now.

THE ACCUSED

I have
accused everyone
in my life of not loving
me enough.

My parents,
my brother, my friends,
and every other person
growing up.

And later,
my best friend, my wife,
my children, and even
my cat.

Imagine that!
But even Jesus, Buddha,
Mohammed, my angels,
and Mary have stood
accused.

No one
loves me, it seems,
and especially not
God.

This is
a terrible state of affairs,
I am sure you agree.
But I must confess that
I am the guilty party.

You see,
when I stop loving me,
I end up accusing everyone
else of not loving
me too.

SANE ENOUGH

We had a fight, last night,
my beloved and I.
As with all our other fights,
I was afraid that this one
would never end.

But by some miracle it did,
and we are back together again.
One of us must have prayed
an extra big prayer,
no doubt.

I'm always astonished at how
—as soon as we stop fighting—
I completely forget what
our fight was about.

From the outside, every fight
looks different; but on the
inside, you can see
that they are all
the same.

One of us forgets temporarily
about the love that we are.
Suddenly we each abandon
love and start acting
insane.

Together, separately, we are
both in pain—without a hope
in hell—until one of us is
sane enough to choose
love again.

INTO THE INNOCENT AGAIN

There is an angel.
An angel who travels with you.
An angel called
Forgiveness.

Your friend,
the angel of forgiveness,
experiences what you
experience.
She knows how you feel.
She knows.

She is the one who meets you
in the darkness.
She knows where to find you.
She is your light.
She is your friend.

The angel of forgiveness
takes you with her into
the innocent again.
She takes you with her,
when you are ready
to go.

Don't look for her over
your head.

You won't find her even
by your side.

She is closer to you than
anything outside of you,
or within.

The angel of forgiveness,
your friend.

NO JUDGMENTS

There
are no judgments in

h
e
a
v
e
n.

EVERY ARGUMENT

every argument
every debate
every war
every hate
every resentment
every grievance
every rivalry
every revenge
must eventually
end in love.

LOVE'S VICTORY

He tried to hide his pain,
but he could not.
He lost his fight with the battle
scars he won at war.

He smoked in bed.
His eyes were bloodshot red.
He tried to hide the empty whisky
bottles in his sock drawer.

He worked for money.
He fought with his boss.
He tried to hide the heartbreak
of a previous divorce.

He was often fierce and cynical.
And he lost the will to live.
But by some miracle, his love
got through to us—my mother,
my brother and me.

The love I feel when I think of him,
twenty-five years on since he died,
now sparkles in my children's eyes.
Dad—this is your victory.

SURRENDER TO LOVE

Admit defeat!
You've tried your best
To love and be loved
But without success

How do you love someone?
So that they know it?
And you know it too?
Here's what to do

Make a petition to love
Go straight to the top
Stop at no other teacher
Listen when love speaks

Love is intelligent
Be a student of love
Ask love to show you how
To love and be loved

WE THREE

I used to think it was just
the two of us. With me
loving you, and you
loving me.

But now I see we are
three. And that love is
doing all the loving
between you
and me.

THE FORGIVENESS PRAYER

Dear God,
I declare today a day of Amnesty
in which I gratefully volunteer to hand
in all of my resentments and grievances
to You. Please help me to handle well
all of the peace, love, happiness,
and success that must
inevitably follow.
Amen.

KNOW LOVE; NO FEAR

Know Love; no fear
Know Joy; no pain
Know Light; no darkness
Know Wholeness; no dis-ease
Know Now; no past
Know Truth; no lies
Know God; no separation
Know Self; no other

A GREAT IDEA

Dear One,
I have a great idea.

Let's love each other.

And keep on loving
until nothing remains
of us—except
love.

Let's disappear
together forever
into love.

BLACK MADONNA

Love
reigns in hell
as it does in
heaven.

Love
shines in darkness
and in the
light.

Love
heals everything
that is not
love.

Love
holds the whole
world in her
hands.

Love
crowns the body
and sanctifies the
soul.

In love,
the sin that never
was, is not
here.

PART IV

LETTING LIFE LOVE YOU

Love whispered in my ear this morning.
"Enjoy this day (it will not come again).
Allow yourself to be loved today in
delightful and surprising ways."
Amen.

When Louise and I wrote our book *Life Loves You*, we examined *basic trust*, a term used by psychologists and philosophers. Basic trust is essential for childhood development and for spiritual growth. We are each born with basic trust. It is not learned; it is only unlearned. It is a *knowing*, which you feel in your bones, that you are loveable and that life loves you. The genesis of creation is Good, with a capital *G*. We are clothed in this Goodness. God is love. The universe is benevolent. There is a Higher Plan. Where there is suffering, help is at hand. The loving hand of the universe is here to guide us.

Louise and I talked about Albert Einstein and the friendly universe theory. The story goes that Einstein once said that the most basic question we must all answer is, "Is the universe a friendly place?" In my research, I stumbled across a book called *Einstein and the Poet*, which documents a conversation over many years between Albert Einstein and the poet William Hermanns. It offers some great insights into Einstein's way of seeing the world.

Einstein often sounded like a poet or a mystic. He advocated having "a holy curiosity." He recognized "an intelligence manifested in nature" and a "marvelous structure behind reality." He saw a "lawful harmony" and a "unified whole." "God is subtle, but he is not malicious," said Einstein.

"Is the universe friendly?" I asked Louise.

"There's only one way to find out," she replied.

"What way is that?"

"Say yes," she said with a smile.

"What do you mean?"

"If you answer no, you'll never find out if the universe is friendly," she said.

"Because if you say no, you won't see it."

"Exactly. But if you say yes, then you might."

"It's all in the answer."

"The answer is in us," said Louise.

As a young boy, I played for long hours by myself in an imaginary world. I wasn't entirely on my own, though. I had two imaginary friends. Mum and Dad knew of them. They were often invited to dinner. I was also best friends with a blackbird who lived in the hedge at the bottom of my garden. He always appeared as soon as I went out to play. My mum was concerned for me, but I couldn't think why. "Aren't you lonely?" she asked. I had a lovely garden (apparently it was small, but so was I). I also had my imagination. I unearthed lots of games and stories out in the garden. I was always in good company even if it appeared I was alone.

As a young man, I learned to be self-sufficient. This happened especially after my mum's bouts of depression increased and my father's alcoholism worsened. The basic trust that had once connected me to the world (both seen and unseen) gave way to a steely self-reliance in adolescence. The world was no longer good; it was only sometimes-good. I had no way of knowing if today was going to be a good day or not. Was Mum going to get out of bed? Was Dad going to fall asleep in the car again? I reinforced my self-reliance after Dad left home and Mum entered a terrible abyss. My life was down to me and me alone, or so it seemed. I had to make my own way in the world now.

Self-reliance only gets you so far, though. It got me through my 20s mostly, but at a price. I was too independent for my own good. My self-reliance had helped me to cultivate willpower, exert extreme self-discipline, and take responsibility for my life. However, it had also cut me off from my friends and distanced me from my heart. My self-reliance was a compensation for my lack of basic trust. I was struggling now to feel good about myself and my life.

One day, I came across a poem by David Whyte. I read it so many times that it became a friend. It's called "Everything Is Waiting for You" and begins, "Your great mistake is to act the drama as if you were alone." Then comes an invitation to "put down the weight of your aloneness and ease into the conversation."

I began to dismantle my self-reliance. I let my friends in on my life. I started to confide in others more. I even asked people for help. I set an intention to become a better receiver. When you're too self-reliant, you're a lousy receiver. I created my own Receiving Journal, in which I recorded daily blessings. The more I did this, the more open I became. Life was less of an effort, and more of a collaboration now. Around this time, I started to write poetry. It happened spontaneously. Before then, I was a bit too tough for poetry. Don't get me wrong; I liked the idea of poetry. I just couldn't get into it. I was too headstrong and full of self-will. Poetry speaks to the heart. I became more engaged with my heart.

Ingrid Goff-Maidoff is a wonderful American poet. I first met Ingrid when she attended my five-day training called Coaching Happiness in San Diego. I remember Louise was also there. The room was full of writers and teachers. It was a great crowd. At the end of the first day, Ingrid gave me a copy of *What Holds Us*, a collection of her poems. I read it in one go that night. *What Holds Us* is full of love songs to a benevolent universe. Her poetry is an invitation to let life love you in all its mysterious and multilingual ways. Over the next few days, I asked Ingrid to read several of her poems to us. One of her short poems is called "God spoke today in flowers." It goes like this:

> God spoke today in flowers,
> and I, who was waiting on words,
> almost missed the conversation.

From time to time, I ask myself, *What is the conversation life is wanting to have with me right now?* I think about Ingrid's poem and how life speaks to us in so many ways. *What is the message I most need to hear today?* Maybe I will hear it in a meditation or in a lyric of a song. *Who will the messenger be?* Maybe an old friend or a butterfly? Here in Part IV, I offer a poem called "Butterflies." It begins "Butterflies are e-mails from heaven." The peacock butterfly, with its cosmic blue eyes on orange wings, has a special significance for me and my family. "Look, it's a Grandma Sally butterfly!" shout Bo and Christopher each time they see one. My mum (Grandma Sally!) speaks to the whole family with the help of butterflies.

In my book *Happiness NOW!*, I included a poem called "A Mad, Forgetful Moment." It was my first published poem. It's here in Part IV. It was inspired by a teaching in *A Course in Miracles* that says, "Into eternity, where all is one, there crept a tiny, mad idea, at which the Son of God remembered not to laugh. In his forgetting [to laugh] did the thought become a serious idea, and possible of both accomplishment and real effects" (T-27.VIII.6:2–3).

What is the tiny, mad idea? It is the thought of separation, which is the great optical delusion here on Earth. It's what causes us to feel alone in the Oneness. It also makes us feel displaced. As if we are always in the wrong place. In truth, we are at home in God, but we are dreaming of exile.

Basic trust says *be present!* It encourages you to pay attention to your life. What you are looking for is where you are. Maybe you are lost. Maybe you have stumbled. Maybe your life's a mess. Maybe you want a better now! Even so, don't run off too soon. Give now another chance, as the present has a gift for you. There is an invitation here. Love will always meet you where you are. I didn't see life this way, not while I was so self-reliant. But when I began to slow down and ease my way into the conversation, I realized I was not alone. Help is available everywhere you are. Hafiz and Daniel Ladinsky teach us in the poem "This Place Where You Are Right Now" that:

This place where you are right now
God circled on a map for you.

Wherever your eyes and arms and heart can move
Against the earth and the sky,
The Beloved has bowed there—

Our Beloved has bowed there knowing
You were coming.

Many of my poems record the ongoing conversation between my ego and my soul. What is the ego? The psychoanalyst Sigmund Freud described the ego as the sense of a separate self. The ego is an image of who we are, but not our true substance. The ego, or persona, is the face we show the world. In T. S. Eliot's poem "The Love Song of J. Alfred Prufrock," the line "to prepare a face to meet the faces that you meet" illustrates this. Freud recognized that our sense of anxious apartness is what causes our ego to be full of mistrust and defensiveness. I studied and taught Freud's defense mechanisms theory for the One Spirit Interfaith Seminary for several years. I shared many of Freud's great insights with my students, including this one that's often attributed to him: "Everywhere I go I find a poet has been there before me."

So how did Freud describe the soul? Freud used the word *psyche* to refer to the soul. *Psyche* is a Greek word meaning "soul" and "breath of life." Nowadays, many Freudians prefer to think of the psyche as "the mind" and equate it with the intellect and with mental processing. However, the original meaning of psyche is most definitely "soul." And our soul is our Original Self, our true substance, which is connected to the Oneness of all things. It houses our Original mind, and it's where our basic trust comes from. The Catholic philosopher Matthew Fox calls the soul our Original Blessing. Buddhists call it our Original Face. W. B. Yeats, the Irish poet, writes in his poem "Before the World Was Made": "I'm looking for the face I had / Before the world was made." The soul, our true nature, is what we are all really searching for.

My poems often come to me when I slow down, in moments of stillness, and while I am meditating. They are an invitation to deepen my inquiry and to be more open to the big Love that is within and everywhere. In my poem "So Sweet," I share how my soul delights in posting love notes in my heart each day. The soul is our guide. It is tuned in to the big Mind, and it recognizes how the loving hand of the universe is always here for us. My poem "White Feathers" is a meditation on how life synchronizes itself to send us signs to guide us on our way.

The soul is here to befriend our ego. The soul can bless us, guide us, and assist us in so many ways, if we allow it to. The Irish poet and mystic John O'Donohue wrote a wonderful collection of meditations and poems called *Benedictus: A Book of Blessings*, and another one called *To Bless the Space Between Us*. When I read John's poems, I feel as if my soul is talking to me. Here's what John had to say about the soul:

> Your soul knows the
> geography of your destiny.
> Your soul alone has the map of
> your future, therefore you can trust
> this indirect, oblique side
> of yourself. If you do, it will
> take you where you need to go,
> but more important it will teach
> you a kindness of rhythm in
> your journey.

A MAD, FORGETFUL MOMENT

There once was a moment,
a mad, forgetful moment, that slipped
past eternity into time.
And in that moment, mad and
forgetful as it was, out of nowhere
an entire world, separate from God,
was dreamed up.

And although it was only a moment,
it felt like forever.
And although it was only a dream,
it felt so real.
In this mad, forgetful world,
the Ocean prayed to God,
"Give me water. I want to be like water."

The Sun, brilliant and bright, would
pray, "Dear God, fill me with light."
And the mighty, powerful, roaming Wind
would plea, "Set me free, set me free."
One time, all of sudden, and I don't quite
know why, Silence began to speak,
"God grant me peace, grant me peace."

Then, Peace itself, fell to its knees,
"Dear God, please, what can I do today
to be more peaceful?"
Now, looking quite perplexed, prayed,
"Dear God, what next?"

Even Eternity began to pray,
"I want to last forever and ever and ever."
Infinity felt small,
"Dear God, help me to grow."
And Life itself, began to cry,
"I don't ever want to die!"

And You and I, the essence of Love,
we cried out for love,
"God, please love me," we prayed.
"God, fill me with love," we prayed.
"God, grant me love."

Mad and forgetful as it was, that
moment in time soon slipped,
tripped, and fell away back into eternity.
It's all over now, save the memory, a
mad, forgetful memory,
it, too, ready for eternity.

BEAUTIFUL OM

God
is silent sometimes,
it's true

But only because
there are not enough
words in the
universe

To convey the love
God feels

For the Beautiful OM
that is You.

JASMINE TEA

I
sip my jasmine
tea.

Flowers
from a cup.

I
am like a
bee.

That
has found divine
nectar.

Somewhere
in me,
God is making
honey.

HALF A POEM

I have written half a poem
here on this page
for you.

Here you can read about the
theory of love—how love made
the universe and the stars,
and that love is what
you are.

The other half of this poem
is written upon
your heart.

Stop reading now,
and tune in to the silence,
to hear what love has
to say.

Every poem is finished off
in the heart, because poetry is,
in essence, listening to the
Voice of Love.

EYE OF THE WHALE

The eye of the whale
is looking into me.

Each time I close my
eyes, I see it.

Watching me.

I disappear into the
eye.

An ocean full of love.

I cannot be what
I am not.

I can only be what
I am.

I am a holy fish.

Swimming between Pisces
and Aquarius.

In bliss consciousness.

A baptism happening to
me, from inside
the eye of the whale.

BUTTERFLIES

Butterflies are e-mails from heaven.
Be sure to pay attention when
A butterfly appears in your garden.
Be still and let it land on you.

Butterflies are sent by loved ones.
They bring tidings from unseen hands.
A flower-bird telegram just for you.
Angel kisses on mandala wings.

Butterflies are full of purpose.
To assist your own metamorphosis.
Through the chrysalis from ego to soul,
Jesus to Christ, Siddhartha to Buddha.

Butterflies are prophets of love.
Your time for resurrection has come.
The dark night will soon be done.
This is your rebirth. It's time to fly.

WHITE FEATHERS

A small white feather
    afloat on the water.
Right here in the middle
    of the wide blue sea.
"See! See! Another one!"
    cry the children.
"This is our sign," affirms the
    captain of our boat.

Navigation by white feathers.
    This is how it happens
out at sea (and on land) when
    you travel without plans.

A turtle asked a seagull
    to lay a spare white feather
    precisely there.

A spotted dolphin had asked
    the turtle to speak to
    the gull.

A whale had asked the dolphin
    to send a message to
    the turtle.

God had originally spoken to
    the whale.

Navigation by white feathers.
    This is how it happens
out at sea (and on land) when
    you let yourself be guided
    by a higher plan.

LOVE'S HAIKU

Love is not a search
Love is not hiding from you
Love is your true guide.

SO SWEET

She is so sweet to me, my soul.

Each day starts with a bang!
Taking breakfast orders downstairs
in the kitchen café.
Doing the school run against
the clock.
Working through another To Do
list, which I'm not on.

It's so nonstop!
But when I do manage to pause,
and pay attention to my life,
I always find a love note waiting
for me, in my heart.

She is so sweet to me, my soul.

Strength, courage, and wisdom.
She goes with me wherever I go.
She is my constant, and she always
tells me what I most need
to know.

My soul, she loves me.
She just can't help it
—posting love notes in my heart—
while I'm fighting traffic, being
busy, doing my day.

She is so sweet to me, my soul.

THE LAST PERSON

Sitting here,
in the dark,
alone with only my
thoughts to keep
me company.

"Will I be the last
person on Earth
to find love?" I
wonder.

"You won't think
thoughts like these
when you stop
hiding from love,"
says the Friend.

Wherever I am,
the Friend knows
where to find me.
I'm always in good
company.

HOLY Q & A

You come to Me only
for answers—but I have
questions too.

One of My questions
may have all the answers
you are looking
for.

Come closer. Let's really
talk. Let's do Q & A.
I can give you questions that
will light up your day.

Today's question is . . . How
will you let life love you
even more today than you
did yesterday?

HOLY OVEN

Sitting here together,
in our morning meditation,
I smell something
cooking.

The silence is a holy oven.

Delicious cookies from the
oven, will soon be
ready to eat.

Let's get some napkins.
We can eat them right
here, on our laps.

For what we are about to
receive, let's be
grateful.

The silence is always
serving up such
wonderful treats.

GREAT BIG KISSES

This morning, as I went to work,
    I looked up at the sky.

I saw clouds passing by,
    that looked like giant lips.

Suddenly I had a spring in
    my step, for I did see

God was blowing great big
    kisses at me.

BREATHE

Love says *breathe.*

Every exhale is
a release.

Every inhale is
a chance to
receive.

THE HOLEY SHOE

"I have a holey shoe," my little
boy told me.
"Let me see," I said, bending
down on one knee.

"Look, it's got a hole in the
sole," he showed me.
"Yes, so I see."

"One of God's angels must
have put it there," he
said.

"Really!"

"Yep. God always does things
like this to make me smile,"
he told me.

"What fun!"

"Angels like to have fun,"
he said, as he poked his finger
all the way through the hole
in his shoe.

ANY NOW WILL DO

Now
is not a moment
in time.

Now
is a state of mind.

Now
is a meeting point
on the path.

Now
is where you meet
yourself at last.

Now
is a place within you
where you are already
happy.

Now
is when everything is
finally forgiven.

Now
is home to the
Prodigal Son.

Now
is your resurrection.

Now
is the immovable spot where
Siddhartha once
sat.

Now
is your enlightenment.
Your "I am that."

Now
is where everything
that is not love
disappears.

Now
is no place for
cynicism, pessimism,
hopes, or fears.

Now
is an invitation from
eternity.

Now is the time to
set yourself free.

Choose any now
and you will see that
all of this is true.

Any now will do.

PART V

BEING THE PRESENCE OF LOVE

Be a sign
for someone today
—a holy confirmation—
that we live in a
benevolent
universe.

"My work is loving the world." This is the first line of Mary Oliver's poem "Messenger." "Do you love this world?" she asks us in another of her poems, "Peonies." Mary Oliver was a nature mystic, an environmentalist, and a poet. She passed away in 2019 while I was writing this book, and I am sorry we never met in person. Her poetry is a constant presence in my life. Each time I read a Mary Oliver poem, I open my eyes, pay attention to my life, and hope to love this world more. Loving the world is a central theme of her work. In her poem "October," she tells us:

Look, I want to love this world
as though it's the last chance I'm ever going to get
to be alive
and know it.

"I want my poetry to be inflammatory!" Mary Oliver told the poet and translator Coleman Barks in a rare interview. Mary preferred to let her poetry speak for itself. She told Coleman how she hoped her poems would be "incendiary devices" that would ignite imagination and action. She didn't just want her poems to console, soothe, and comfort people. "I want my poetry to change things," she said. Mary was an activist. She used poetry to ask big questions, challenge our thinking, engage our hearts, and, ultimately, make sure we each create something beautiful in the world. In her poem "Franz Marc's Blue Horses," she wrote:

> Maybe the desire to make something beautiful
> is the piece of God that is inside each of us.

My poem "Love's Question," which makes an appearance here in Part V, is a thank-you to Mary Oliver. Like many of Mary's poems, it asks a question of us. "Love's Question" is a short poem that takes only a moment to read, but your reply to it might take a lifetime. The poetry I like best asks for a response from the reader. A poem is only ever half a poem until we do something with it. A poem ignites something in us. A poem is a call to arms.

Maya Angelou was also a poet and an activist. I interviewed Maya three times. The first time was on Valentine's Day, and we talked about love, naturally. I started by quoting Maya to Maya! She once said, "Love builds up the broken wall and straightens the crooked path. Love keeps the stars in the firmament and imposes rhythm on the ocean tides. Each of us is created of it and I suspect each of us was created for it." I shared with Maya some ideas from my book *Loveability*, which was hot off the press. We talked about love as our true identity, love as our purpose, and love as the essential action of our life. "Love is a great doing!" Maya told me.

Several months later, I interviewed Maya again shortly after Nelson Mandela's death. Maya had written a tribute poem called "His Day Is Done." I asked Maya for some insights into Nelson Mandela and his inspiring life. "He loved everybody the same," she said. Maya told me how Nelson showed the same love and respect to everyone regardless of their status, skin color, politics, or religion. "He showed the same kindness to my guest, who was a Head of State, to my gardener and my housekeeper," she told me. The final lines of "His Day Is Done" read:

We will not forget you.
We will not dishonor you.
We will remember and be glad
That you lived among us
That you taught us
And
That you loved us
All!

Maya and I talked about how Nelson Mandela modeled a love-centered leadership. Love was at the heart of his politics. He wore an international heart. His message was not only for one nation, one race, or one side. He was an activist in the highest sense because his work was an expression of love-in-action for all of humanity.

Maya wrote seven autobiographies. Her first was *I Know Why the Caged Bird Sings*, one of her most loved works. She started out by looking for love, as we all do. Writing about her heartbreaks helped her to overcome them. She became the love she was looking for. Maya, like Nelson Mandela, wore an international heart too. She discovered a love that does not discriminate. She sided with a higher power that is greater than the world. She taught us that "love recognizes no barriers. It jumps hurdles, leaps fences, penetrates walls to arrive at its destination full of hope."

Maya loved the world. At the end of one my interviews with Maya, I thanked her for being a voice for Love in our world and for being the presence of love to us all.

Tom Carpenter introduced me to the term "the presence of love." We've talked about the meaning of the presence of love and also the practice of it, since we first met 20-something years ago. Tom was the first person to teach me that the aim of life is not to search for love, but to see that love is everywhere. He helped me to open my eyes, to pay attention, and to look more closely at what is always right here. I remember once telling Tom, "Love is woven into the fabric of life." "No," he replied, "love is the fabric of life. There would be no life without love."

In my poem "Love Is Gravity," I explore the idea that there is nowhere where love is not. We exist in a field of love, in a way that's similar for birds that fly in the sky and fish that swim in the sea. From this point of view, there is no emptiness. The world is full of love.

We do have to practice emptiness, though. Emptiness is the practice of letting go of everything that is not love—the optical delusion of separation, our belief in sin, our lack of self-worth, our secondhand knowledge, our old grievances, the habit of judging, and everything else that is not love.

The term "presence of love" recognizes both that love is always present and that our original nature is the presence of love. In a short film I made with Tom, called *The Presence of Love*, Tom says, "We were created in love from love. That's what life is. There really is no purpose for the presence of life without the presence of love. Life was given to us to express what we are, which is the presence of love." The invitation here is to see that your goal is not to search for love; it is to recognize that you are made of love. Your original mind is full of love. Love is the heart of who you are. Love is your spiritual DNA.

In *A Course in Miracles*, which is the book that brought Tom and me together, we are encouraged to identify with love. In one of the daily meditations in the *Course*, Lesson 229, you will find these words: "I seek my own Identity, and find it in these words: 'Love, which created me, is what I am.' Now need I seek no more. Love has prevailed." In another passage, the *Course* states,

> Identify with love, and you are safe.
> Identify with love, and you are home.
> Identify with love, and find your Self.
> (W-pII.5.5:6–8)

Love is our daily spiritual practice. First, we declare we are willing to be a loving presence in the world today. We affirm that love is our true identity. Love is our I AM. Next, we dedicate the day to love. My poem "Love Dedication" speaks to the importance of this. When we dedicate our day to love, we open ourselves up to higher realms of imagination and creativity. Then, we invite the loving hand of the universe to guide us throughout the day. Love is intelligent. Love is our GPS. Love will show us how to love and be loved and how to live this day. We let love lead the way.

Your spiritual practice is love-in-action. Love isn't just sitting on a meditation cushion. Sitting may help you to tune in to love. However, the next part of your spiritual practice is to show up and be a loving presence in your day. Remember, you can ask Love to show you how to do this. With Love's help, you can be an instrument of love in whatever you do today. Love-in-action is all about the loving presence you bring to your everyday tasks, like making breakfast, doing the school run, sending a text, serving a customer, conducting a board meeting, standing on your yoga mat, kissing your children good night, and brushing your teeth before bedtime.

Everyone talks about "small acts of love," but there's really no such thing. With love, there are no small acts! Every loving action is maximal. By simply watering a flower, and doing it with love, you have started a movement in consciousness that has no end. How so? Love belongs to the Oneness. In the Oneness, a single act of love touches everyone. Every act of love is equally valuable. Why? Because it's not about the action; it's about the love. With every love-in-action you perform, you remind yourself that you are the love you once searched for.

START OF SOMETHING WONDERFUL

It's time to do
nothing.

Start doing
nothing immediately.

Make doing
nothing your work
today.

Do nothing,
and do not even make
it a technique.

This doing nothing is
a divine opportunity.

It takes you to the heart of now.
A meeting place, where your
Soul waits for you.

Doing nothing,
in its purest form,
is receptivity.

Your non-action draws to
you extra
possibility.

Doing nothing is the start
of something
wonderful.

It's what an orchestra does
to sound the first note
of a symphony.

It's what each of us must do
if we are to let the divine
act through us.

Doing nothing
is holy work.

Out of the nothingness,
a new adventure
begins.

Starting
from
now.

LOVE'S INSTRUMENT

I am a pencil in God's hands.

I am here to write Love Letters from God to
everyone in the world.

God is ready to write and therefore so am I.

I sit patiently before God and listen
for the thoughts of God.

I ask God to remove any imagined blocks to
writing now.

I meet every fear with love.

I find it easier than expected to write
because God does the work.

All I do is listen.

And take notes.

And enjoy the
process.

LOVE NOTES

The world is full
of paper
To make out checks
Print receipts
Roll up cigarettes
Make confetti
Draw pictures
And write love notes
—lots and lots of
love notes.

LOVE DEDICATION

Before you dedicate your life
to a person, a marriage, a family;
to a corporation, a political party,
a peace campaign;
to a religion, a revolution, a
spiritual path;
make one other dedication first.

First dedicate yourself to LOVE.
Decide to let Love be your
intention, your purpose and
your point.
And then let Love inspire you,
support you, and guide you
in every other dedication
you make thereafter.

LOVE IS GRAVITY

Love is gravity.
It brings you down to
Earth.

You did not fall.
You were sent.
You chose to be here.
You gave your consent.

Love brings you down
from your head,
into your heart and
into your hips.

Love helps you take your
place in this world.
To find your feet.
To stand upright
on solid ground.

Love stops you floating off.
So that you can be here.
In the low places.
Doing your holy work.

An undercover Love Agent.
The Presence of Love.
You're here to ensure
that there is nowhere
where love is not.

DIVINE FEMININE

I
have been
pregnant
ever since the
beginning.

My
body is
Mary.

I
will be
pregnant
for all my days
on Earth.

My
mind is
Joseph.

I
am birthing
holiness
for
Aquarius.

My Soul
is a
child of
God.

The
Christ
is alive in
me.

THREE ANGELS

I once overheard two angels
deep in conversation.

They were contemplating the
finer details of metaphysics
and of heaven.

At one point, Angel 1 asked
Angel 2, "If you had to
choose between light or love,
what would you do?"

Suddenly, I saw a third angel
in the sky. "That's easy!" I
heard her cry.

"I would choose love," said
Angel 3. When asked why,
she replied, "Because love
is not afraid of the
dark."

YOUR LOVE IS A GIFT

It is because the world is so full of suffering,
that your happiness is a gift.
It is because the world is STILL so full of poverty,
that your wealth is a gift.
It is because the world can be so unfriendly,
that your smile is a gift.
It is because the world is so full of war,
that your peace of mind is a gift.
It is because the world is in such despair,
that your hope and optimism is a gift.
It is because the world is so afraid,
that your love is a gift.

LOVE'S QUESTION

If
you were to accept
that your only work today
is to love the world,
how, do you imagine,
would you
begin?

NEW KIND OF POLITICS

I'm voting for a new kind of politics.
Based not on opposition, but on imagination.
A politics with an international heart.
A climate change from fear to love.
With a defense budget for trees,
and a Ministry for Bees.
A new flag for Planet Earth.
An end to debt economies.
No need for charities.
No third world. Just one world.
Where leaders who love the most
always win the majority
vote.

DISAPPEARING INTO LOVE

When they ask you what is your
religion, tell them that it is
love.

And if they ask you what is your
politics, tell them that it is
also love.

If they ask you what that means,
you can tell them your
philosophy is love.

If they want to know anything
else about you, tell them your
favorite occupation is
loving.

And don't forget to tell them
that your nationality is
love.

And that even your blood
group is love.

Not everyone will stick around
to hear what you say next,
but fear not.

Family and friends may get busy
so as to pretend to forget what
you just said.

It'd drive them crazy now to know
that their blood group is also love,
that their nationality is love,
and that the real work of their
life is love.

One day they will give in, and then
their philosophy will be love,
their politics will be love,
and their religion will be love.

Love gets us all in the end.
We all of us disappear back into
love eventually.

JUST ONE MORE THING

If this is it,
and our time is up,
I'd pray the biggest prayer
I ever did pray.
I'd ask for ten more seconds,
for one more breath,
so that I could say to
you again

Thank you for everything.
I love you.

ACKNOWLEDGMENTS

Thank you to my family. You are my muses. Thank you, Hollie Holden, for your love of poetry. From the beginning, we've been writing and reciting poems to each other. Thank you, Bo Holden, for your lyrical soul, your singing and your creativity. Thank you, Christopher Holden, for your big heart and your big-fun-adventure spirit. Thank you to my mother Sally, my father Alex, my brother David, and especially to my great uncle, Derek Hill, whose life as an artist gave me inspiration and hope.

Thank you to Tom and Linda Carpenter, Louise Hay, Maya Angelou, Helen Schucman, Eileen Caddy, Dorothy Maclean and to all the spiritual teachers I've met along the way. Thank you, Daniel Ladinsky, for introducing me to Hafiz. Thanks also for writing e-mails the same way you write poems. Thank you, Mary Oliver, for helping me to pay attention to my life. Thank you, David Whyte, for encouraging me to remember what is real. Thank you, Ingrid Goff-Maidoff, for showing me how to listen to God's conversation.

A great joy of friendship is sharing poems. With each of these friends, I can easily recall one or many "poem moments" together. Thank you, Lizzie and Matthew Winn, Charlie and Marysia Prior, Meggan Watterson, Liz Wenner, Russ Hudson, Cheryl Richardson, Michael Gerrish, Kyle Gray, David Hamilton, Rebecca Campbell, Amy Kiberd, Declan Kiberd, Nina Hirlaender, Mary and Ron Hulnick, Marianne Williamson, Venetia David, Richard Dunkerley, and the Alternatives team, Nicola Coombe, Elmer Postle, Jo Van Zyl, Adele Napier, John Willoner, Sylvia Black, Jonathan Caddy, Jackee Holder, Sean Patrick, Diane Berke, Peter Dewey, Anne Burkett, Shawn Gallaway, Chuck and Lency Spezzano, Marika Borg, Julia Dvinskaya, Margli Matthews, Colette Baron-Reid, Wayne Dyer, Brian Weiss, Avanti Kumar, Raina Nahar, Robert Norton, Sue Boyd, Candy Talbot, Avril Carson, Charlie Shand, Shawn Gallaway, Tim Wheater, Michael Furber, Caroline Myss, Andrew Harvey, Winny & Kees van de Velden, Ahlea Khadro, Deena Fadel,

Katey Roberts, Diane Haworth, Kisser Paludan, Deborah & Gene Threadgill Egerton, Aileen Socrates, Helen Bradley, Donna Bond, Linda Connor, Randi Suskin, Ellen Kristine Kraakenes, and Nicola Albini, to name a few!

A big thank you to Laura Samuel and Brenton Hughes for helping me safeguard the time for my poetry. The morning belongs to the mystic; the afternoon belongs to everyone else!

Thank you to Sabine Weeke for the vital part you played in bringing this book to life and thank you also for the idea of writing half a poem.

Thank you to the Hay House team. Thank you, Louise Hay, for being a loving presence in my life. Thank you, Reid Tracy, for giving me such a rich canvas to paint on. Thank you, Patty Gift, for being a wonderful friend and editor. Thank you, Anne Barthel, Sally Mason, and Lisa Bernier, for your skillful and sensitive editing. Thank you to Tricia Breidenthal and your team for your creative art direction.

Thank you to the WME Agency, to Jamie Carr, and to my agent Jennifer Rudolph Walsh.

ABOUT THE AUTHOR

Robert Holden's work on psychology and spirituality has been featured on *Oprah*, *Good Morning America*, a PBS special *Shift Happens!*, and in two major BBC-TV documentaries, *The Happiness Formula* and *How to Be Happy*. Robert runs a Love-Centered Mastermind program that trains psychologists and educators in a love-based approach to therapy and counseling. He is on the guest faculty of the University of Santa Monica, which teaches a soul-centered approach to psychology. He is a student of *A Course in Miracles* and a Patron of the Miracle Network. He is a student of the Enneagram and teaches workshops on *Love and the Enneagram*. He regularly leads spiritual retreats to places like Jerusalem, Findhorn, Galilee, Assisi, Montserrat, and Glastonbury.

Robert is a best-selling author of 10 books including: *Happiness NOW!*, *Shift Happens!*, *Authentic Success*, *Be Happy*, *Loveability*, and *Life Loves You* (co-written with Louise Hay). *Finding Love Everywhere* is his first book of poetry. Robert writes a weekly newsletter called *Shift Happens!* He is an official contributor to Oprah.com and also for the *Chicken Soup for the Soul* series. Robert has hosted a weekly show for 10 years on Hay House Radio called *Shift Happens!* Website: www.robertholden.com

HAY HOUSE TITLES
OF RELATED INTEREST

YOU CAN HEAL YOUR LIFE, the movie, starring Louise Hay & Friends
(available as a 1-DVD program, an expanded 2-DVD set,
and an online streaming video)
Learn more at www.hayhouse.com/louise-movie

THE SHIFT, the movie, starring Dr. Wayne W. Dyer
(available as a 1-DVD program, an expanded 2-DVD set,
and an online streaming video)
Learn more at www.hayhouse.com/the-shift-movie

❖ ❖ ❖

*THE ART OF EXTREME SELF-CARE: 12 Practical and
Inspiring Ways to Love Yourself More,*
by Cheryl Richardson

*HAPPINESS IS THE WAY: How to Reframe Your Thinking and Work
with What You Already Have to Live the Life of Your Dreams,*
by Dr. Wayne W. Dyer

LIFE LOVES YOU: 7 Spiritual Practices to Heal Your Life, by Louise Hay &
Robert Holden

*SUPER ATTRACTOR: Methods for Manifesting a Life beyond Your Wildest
Dreams,* by Gabrielle Bernstein

All of the above are available at your local bookstore,
or may be ordered by contacting Hay House (see next page).

❖ ❖ ❖

We hope you enjoyed this Hay House book. If you'd like to receive
our online catalog featuring additional information on Hay House
books and products, or if you'd like to find out more about the
Hay Foundation, please contact:

Hay House, Inc., P.O. Box 5100, Carlsbad, CA 92018-5100
(760) 431-7695 or (800) 654-5126
(760) 431-6948 (fax) or (800) 650-5115 (fax)
www.hayhouse.com® • www.hayfoundation.org

———

Published in Australia by: Hay House Australia Pty. Ltd.,
18/36 Ralph St., Alexandria NSW 2015
Phone: 612-9669-4299 • *Fax:* 612-9669-4144
www.hayhouse.com.au

Published in the United Kingdom by: Hay House UK, Ltd.,
The Sixth Floor, Watson House, 54 Baker Street, London W1U 7BU
Phone: +44 (0)20 3927 7290 • *Fax:* +44 (0)20 3927 7291
www.hayhouse.co.uk

Published in India by: Hay House Publishers India,
Muskaan Complex, Plot No. 3, B-2, Vasant Kunj, New Delhi 110 070
Phone: 91-11-4176-1620 • *Fax:* 91-11-4176-1630
www.hayhouse.co.in

———

**Access New Knowledge.
Anytime. Anywhere.**

Learn and evolve at your own pace
with the world's leading experts.

www.hayhouseU.com

Listen. Learn. Transform.

Listen to the audio version of this book for FREE!

Today, life is more hectic than ever—so you deserve on-demand and on-the-go solutions that inspire growth, center your mind, and support your well-being.

Introducing the *Hay House Unlimited Audio* mobile app. Now you can listen to this book (and countless others)—without having to restructure your day.

With your membership, you can:

- Enjoy over 30,000 hours of audio from your favorite authors.
- Explore audiobooks, meditations, Hay House Radio episodes, podcasts, and more.
- Listen anytime and anywhere with offline listening.
- Access exclusive audios you won't find anywhere else.

Try FREE for 7 days!